Bb Trumpet

More Great Hymns

Instrumental Solos for Worship

Selected by James Curnow

Audio Access Included

T0085570

Contents

PLAYBACK+
Speed • Pitch • Balance • Loop

To access audio, visit:
www.halleonard.com/mylibrary

3885-6681-6128-3350

ISBN 978-90-431-2106-4

CURNOW®
MUSIC

EXCLUSIVELY DISTRIBUTED BY

HAL•LEONARD®

For all works contained herein:
Unauthorized copying, arranging, adapting, recording, Internet posting, public performance,
or other distribution of the music in this publication is an infringement of copyright.
Infringers are liable under the law.

Visit Hal Leonard Online at
www.halleonard.com

Contact us:
Hal Leonard
7777 West Bluemound Road
Milwaukee, WI 53213
Email: info@halleonard.com

In Europe, contact:
Hal Leonard Europe Limited
42 Wigmore Street
Marylebone, London, W1U 2RN
Email: info@halleonardeurope.com

In Australia, contact:
Hal Leonard Australia Pty. Ltd.
4 Lentara Court
Cheltenham, Victoria, 3192 Australia
Email: info@halleonard.com.au

More Great Hymns
B♭ Trumpet

Arranged by:
Stephen Bulla
Douglas Court
James Curnow
Timothy Johnson
Kevin Norbury

Copyright © 2004 by Curnow Music Press, Inc. P.O. Box 142, Wilmore, KY 40390, USA

More Great Hymns

INTRODUCTION

This collection of some of the world's greatest hymns was created for, and is dedicated to, my good friend and musical colleague, Philip Smith, Principal Trumpet, New York Philharmonic Orchestra. The goal of these arrangements is to allow instrumentalists the opportunity to give praise and adoration to God through their musical abilities.

Though these arrangements have been written for trumpet, with Phil in mind, cued notes have been added to allow players at many different levels and on various different instruments to perform them. They are playable on all instruments (C Treble Clef, B♭ Treble Clef, E♭, F or Bass Clef) by simply purchasing the appropriate book that coincides with the key of their instrument.

The piano accompaniment book has been written to work with all instruments. An accompaniment track for each hymn is included with the online audio (which is included with all of the solo books), should a piano accompanist not be available. The audio also includes a sample performance of each arrangement with a soloist. Appropriate tuning notes have been added to allow the soloists the opportunity to adjust their intonation to the intonation of the compact disc accompaniment.

More Great Hymns is the second book in this series. The first book, *Great Hymns,* is also available through your favorite music dealer. It includes arrangements of the following hymns:

All Creatures Of Our God And King
Praise To The Lord, The Almighty
Be Thou My Vision
O Worship The King
Joyful, Joyful, We Adore Thee
Brethren, We Have Met To Worship
We Gather Together
I Sing The Mighty Power Of God
A Mighty Fortress Is Our God
All Hail The Power

May you enjoy using this collection and find it useful in extending your musical ministry.

Kindest regards,

James Curnow
President

More Great Hymns

PHILIP SMITH
Principal Trumpet
NEW YORK PHILHARMONIC

Philip Smith joined the New York Philharmonic as Co-Principal Trumpet in October 1978, and assumed the position of Solo Principal Trumpet in June 1988. His early training was provided at The Salvation Army, and continued under the training of his father, Derek Smith. He is a graduate of The Juilliard School, having studied with Edward Treutel and William Vacchiano, former Principal Trumpet of the New York Philharmonic. In January of 1975, while still at Juilliard, Mr. Smith was appointed to the Chicago Symphony Orchestra by Sir Georg Solti.

Mr. Smith has appeared regularly as soloist, recitalist, chamber orchestra performer and clinician. He has been featured as a soloist with the Philharmonic in over 75 performances under such conductors as Zubin Mehta, Kurt Masur, Erich Leinsdorf, Leonard Bernstein, Neeme Jarvi and Bram Tovey. Highlights have included the World Premiere of Joseph Turrin's Concerto with the New York Philharmonic, its subsequent European Premiere with the Leipzig Gewandhaus Orchestra, the U.S. Premiere of Jacques Hetu's Concerto, the World Premiere (2000) of Lowell Liebermann's Concerto, and the World Premiere (2003) of Siegfried Matthus' Double Concerto for Trumpet, Trombone and Orchestra. He has been a guest soloist with the Edmonton Symphony, Newfoundland Symphony, Columbus (Indiana) Symphony, Pensacola (Florida) Symphony, Hartford (Connecticut) Symphony, and Beaumont (Texas) Symphony.

Mr. Smith has also appeared with many symphonic wind ensembles including the United States "President's Own" Marine Band, La Philharmonic Des Vents Des Quebec, the Hanover Wind Symphony, the Ridgewood Concert Band, and many major university wind ensembles. He appeared at the College Band Directors National

Association Convention in Austin, Texas for the World Premiere (1999) of Turrin's "Chronicles" with the University of New Mexico Wind Ensemble.

An avid brass band enthusiast, Mr. Smith has been guest soloist with the United States Army Brass Band, Goteborg Brass (Sweden), Black Dyke Mills and Ridged Containers Bands (Britain), Hannaford Street Silver Band and Intrada Brass (Canada), and numerous American and Salvation Army Brass Bands. He appeared as featured soloist at the 1996 British Open Brass Band Championships in Manchester, England.

Mr. Smith is on the faculty at The Juilliard School and has appeared as recitalist and clinician at the Caramoor International Music Festival, Grand Teton Music Festival, Swiss Brass Week, Breman (Germany) Trumpet Days, Oslo (Norway) Trumpet Week, Harmony Ridge (Vermont) Festival, Scotia Festival of Music and numerous International Trumpet Guild conferences.

Mr. Smith has performed and recorded with the Canadian Brass, the Empire Brass, Chamber Music Society of Lincoln Center, Mostly Mozart Orchestra, Bargemusic and NY Virtuosi Chamber Symphony. His solo recordings include "Contest Solos" produced by the International Trumpet Guild, "Fandango" featuring New York Philharmonic Principal Trombonist Joseph Alessi and the University of New Mexico Wind Symphony (Summit), "My Song of Songs" with the New York Staff Band of the Salvation Army (Triumphonic), Copland's "Quiet City" (Deutsche Grammophone), New York Legends (CALA), Orchestral Excerpts for Trumpet (Summit), Ellen Taaffe Zwilich's Concerto for Trumpet and Five Instruments (New World), Bach's Brandenburg Concerto No. 2 (Koch), Walton's Façade (Arabesque), and The Trump Shall Resound and Repeat the Sounding Joy (Heritage/Resounding Praise).

Mr. Smith has recently been involved in a series of projects with Curnow Music Press, publishing music arrangements with demonstration CD's. These include "Great Hymns" for Trumpet, Piano and Organ, "Concert Studies" for Trumpet, and "Great Carols" for Trumpet, Piano and Organ. He has also been featured in a similar project entitled "Total Trumpet" featuring trumpet studies written by Michael Davis and demonstrated by Randy Brecker, Jim Hynes and Philip Smith, published by Hip-Bone Music.

Mr. Smith and his wife perform with their Gospel group, Resounding Praise, throughout North America. They have two adult children and live in New Jersey.

1. HOW FIRM A FOUNDATION

Traditional
Arr. **Stephen Bulla** (ASCAP)

 Copyright © 2004 by **Curnow Music Press, Inc.**

Bb Trumpet

2. AMAZING GRACE

Traditional
Arr. **James Curnow** (ASCAP)

Copyright © 2004 by **Curnow Music Press, Inc.**

3. SOFTLY AND TENDERLY

Will L. Thompson
Arr. Timothy Johnson (ASCAP)

Copyright © 2004 by Curnow Music Press, Inc.

4. O FOR A THOUSAND TONGUES TO SING

Charles G. Glaser
Arr. **Douglas Court** (ASCAP)

Copyright © 2004 by **Curnow Music Press, Inc.**

B♭ Trumpet

Johann Sebastian Bach
5. JESU, JOY OF MAN'S DESIRING

Arr. **Stephen Bulla** (ASCAP)

Copyright © 2004 by Curnow Music Press, Inc.

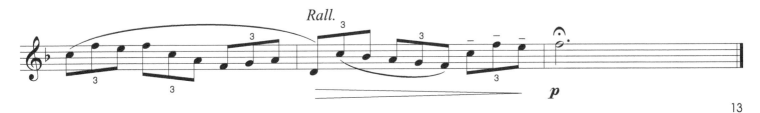

Bb Trumpet

6. HOLY GOD, WE PRAISE THY NAME

From "Katholisches Gesangbuch", 1774   Arr. **Kevin Norbury** (ASCAP)

Copyright © 2004 by **Curnow Music Press, Inc.**

B♭ Trumpet

7. EASTER GLORY

Christ Arose and Christ the Lord Is Risen Today

Robert Lowry
Charles Wesley
Arr. **James Curnow** (ASCAP)

Copyright © 2004 by **Curnow Music Press, Inc.**

Bb Trumpet

8. HOLY,HOLY,HOLY

John B. Dykes
Arr. **Douglas Court** (ASCAP)

Copyright © 2004 by **Curnow Music Press, Inc.**

Bb Trumpet

9. LEAD ON, O KING ETERNAL

Henry T. Smart

Arr. **Timothy Johnson** (ASCAP)

Copyright © 2004 by **Curnow Music Press, Inc.**

Bb Trumpet

10. MY FAITH LOOKS UP TO THEE

Lowell Mason
Arr. **James Curnow** (ASCAP)

Copyright © 2004 by **Curnow Music Press, Inc.**